double-barreled bible
a poet's quest for the almighty

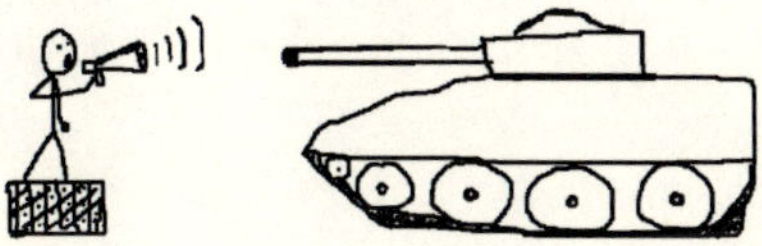

Thank You

What others say about double-barreled bible

"Jordan uses words the same way the old masters used paint. His poetry is brilliant, naked, and powerful."

~ *Patricia Briggs, #1 New York Times Best Selling Author*

***

"Scalpel sharp yet elegantly insightful, Jordan's poetry dissects the ego even as it expands the heart."

~ *Ellen Tomaszewski, Editor, Etcetera Press and author of My Blindy Girl—a mother's journey through achromatopsia.*

***

"Jordan Chaney is an extraordinary young talent, poised on the edge of becoming well known. *double-barreled bible* is an important first work in what will surely be an extensive vita. When he says, 'i feel like …i'm being drawn and quartered by the force of four horses pulling towards the four corners of earth's unforgiving fortress,' I know exactly where he is standing. He understands your dilemma. Jordan Chaney wants to heal you. Let him."

~*Bart Baxter, 1994 MTV Poetry Grand Slam Winner*

double-barreled
bible

a poet's quest for the almighty

Jordan Chaney

All rights reserved.

double-barreled bible
a poet's quest for the almighty

Copyright © 2009, 2010, 2011
Jordan Chaney

This material is copyrighted.
No part of this book may be reproduced, copied,
or transmitted in any form without
written consent from the author.

ISBN: 978-0-9785160-9-3
LOC Number: 2009934554

Etcetera Press
Richland, WA
United States of America
www.etcpress.info

etcetera press

Author Jordan Chaney

table of contents

foreword—viii
preface—ix

chapter 1 toasting with Molotov cocktails—1
mission statement—2
picket sign—4
Columbus sailed a warship—8
sweet guile—11
ill design—12
gun powder—13
1001—14

chapter 2 birdcages—15
fragile things song—16
fragile things—17
half-breed—20
blueberry muffin—23
lost soul—27
phone conversation with a friend—28
united states of mind—30
idyll of Vegas—32

chapter 3 fire poker to the back—35
beaten—36
i come from bad— 37
lemon tree (essay) — 41
Jerome's war— 43
wounded— 46
yellow woman— 49
lighthouses— 51

chapter 4 meditating on the sun—55
fortune—56
she's fly—58
insatiable—61
magnanimous you—62
postcards of heaven—63
world hunger—64
meditation with Rama—65

chapter 7 transformation—67
clairvoyance—68
mind power—69
gigantic—70
awakening—71
i too am the lotus—73
light—74
song of the God Self—78

final note (art of language)—80
glossary—82

Acknowledgements—92

foreword

I write in the lounge car of an Amtrak train barreling eastward down double tracks, north of the Bible Belt. As I ease between wakefulness and sleep, I imagine this book picked up carefully from a hotel room nightstand. Guiding and consoling the devout and the lonely.

I imagine it snatched from under a convenience store counter, loaded with succinctly encapsulated shells of compassionate wisdom, prepared to propel forth, indiscriminately spraying, indiscriminately saving the clerk, robber and passersby. I imagine this book rolled up in the back pocket of a traveling bluesman hitching a ride at the crossroads of where we've been and what we can become.

In fact, I first became acquainted with Jordan Chaney and his work when he and I met at a particular spot on the crossroads. We met at the splatter spot on the road where objects that think they are rejected from heaven are sent to slip through the cracks, find one another and remind one another to burst back through the brain's sub terrain in rapid frightening ascents. As we've been running down parallel tracks ever since, I crane my neck up and ahead to catch a glimpse of billowing brilliance.

~ Orion Baker
March, 2008

preface

This is how my book came to be.

Imagine walking out on an old rickety pier towards a blurry sun the world vanishing behind you. The person you thought you were ages then dies, breathing life into your undying self. You vibrate with fearlessness and peace. You take comfort in the certainty and awareness of your immortality. You look down only to see the pier has long since disappeared from beneath you, you have long since detached from the limitations of the body as well. You peer out to look for the blurry sun but can only see an old world and a fragile pier fading in the distance. You've become the sun.

This is transformation.

i invite you to walk with me…

double barreled bible

this book will change you

chapter 1
toasting with Molotov cocktails

mission statement

i am
not a big fish in a small pond
i'm more like a great whale splashing in a kiddy pool
flapping and gasping in all the air in the whole atmosphere
leaving all those who hear me breathless

i bring a divine message
that caresses your higher essence
if you feel you've been disconnected from the heavens
i'll sever the sixes and replace them with sevens

that's the mind body and soul plus the four life elements

marching like elephants
a solar body wrapped in melanin
like a golden child trapped in a lower class dwelling
in search of his own relevance

until reverence is shown/shone
my words float like smoke to unroll the souls
cobbed in the webs that spiders sure have woven

i render the golden shine
from the honey stored in
the honey combs of our minds that
have been stolen

i sting bees back
in a war for the only
inheritance that God has bestowed
a bright being

a bright light
a stowaway punching holes
in the bellies of slave boats

entertained while watching them sink like stones

to prove that in the afterlife beyond the coral reefs of sleep
that life exists only within the parameters of what we
think

and i think
we are rising out of a crimson tide
kicking our feet
through the stardust
on a cosmic shore storming the beaches
in a spiritual war to breed peace
rescuing our teachers from seeking
half truth behind our enemies minds!

my spine reflecting a vine connecting to concord grapes

call me a tree hugger
blasting coconuts from the trunks of palm trees
aiming for a new world in a heavenly outer space
i've disrupted the transatlantic trade and am now surfing
a radio wave through time and space to find my way home

vibrating on ohm/om
until these poems are well known
i'll flap my tail and sink the slave-ship
as a fisher of men who uses word as tackle and bait
piously executing my mission to make statements
i fight wars with breath words and language

picket sign

if trees and bees become extinct
then so will human beings and their dreams
and countless other beautiful things
i confess i'm in love with your geometry
because even atomically you charm me with flutes
and have me shopping for mushroom-cloud-proof-suits
and the news is a constant bombardment of war talk
and stock drops and the disarmament of enemies who
for centuries hunt like a culture of vultures next to bibles
with fuses burning illusions while our youth is more
worried about music and there's a militant spiritual
awareness that flares when we shake sticks at their
petroleum hives and they reply by hijacking planes
with little knives out of our friendly skies and this cycle
continues and escalates then decorates the fleeting decades
with puppeteering warlords that engage in ignorant intercourse
and forewarn each other of nuclear weather

then play chess with the flesh of our young

darkness should meditate on the sun
trees and bees are sunshine breathing beings so it's not just
human beings that desire peace it's also the soil the river the sky
and the beast but the war that war headed for neglects insects and
has an audience that's applauding when train wrecks occur

i understand this may sound absurd
because the majority of mankind
say they oppose this war but it's still mankind's taxes
that fuel these actions against these freedom fighters
    or terrorists
that are creating world wide hysteria all while on your
    bumper sticker
you proclaim God should bless America when America
    starts wars
over natural resources and then hoards them when it
    comes to import
and export them

thus far this idea alone is on a throne of its own
it is a picket sign with the split personality of a Molotov
    cocktail
each word is its glass shrapnel this is a fuse for
    a revolution to
dissolve self confusion a subtle solution woven together
with the alchemy of tear gas and roses that composes the
finest contrast to put worlds of words in motion, this
    should be
cremated and its ashes used as fertilizer
    for future freedom fighters
that fuel righteous fires with tongue

darkness should meditate on the sun
this should be read and wide spread throughout slums
and blood banks and engraved upon prison shanks even
at food banks this scroll shall be found and read out loud

my senses won't be censored unblock my mouth

double-barreled bible

this poem is merely a vapor of an ancient soul of a lanky
convict malnourished but still digging a hole through
    stone
out of hell with his fingernails because his freedom fails at
    home
and i'm well known like tenements and grass shacks in 3rd
    world
countries i'm a battle axe gift wrapped in pimp slaps back
    at
political pimps that entrap the global lower class of God's
    second half
and then charge into war skin headed and bare back

i don't think nations that have amnesia should be allowed
    to bear double-barreled bibles

loaded with verses that have been perverted its fetal
    corpse is hidden in
churches and even though it is rotting it is still giving birth
    and clotting
the universe in the form of habits and political cabinets
    especially on
this end where its soft skin is marbling and startling the
    passers-by like
you and i who have to share this soon to be mushroom-
    cloud tinted sky

and then you may think the whole world is at war but it's
    not it's only
a species of mental weaklings who are feeding on these
    violent feastings
because the world will never become a panhandling bum
    with unreal eyes

of onyx that seem to shun the blasphemies and
        catastrophes of humanity's mind
which motors humanity's gun

this poem could be a picket sign or these pages used as a
        fuse for a cocktail bomb
to be hurled into the miasmic throne or noxious world of
        the political boys and
political girls

who might smother the mother who holds the womb
        which could one day
soon give birth to the child with peace so mild and sweet
        fires would freeze
and you would crawl for miles on knees just to get a
        glimpse of the golden
curls on this great sheep

Columbus sailed a warship

if you're trying to find your self worth
inside of a church in a search
to end the cycle of death & birth
hell it might be worth it
if you're not forced to forfeit
your natural fortune
that contains infinite sage-like worth
that's already worthy of worship…

i know that Columbus sailed a warship

classrooms try
to disguise this lie

like it was something more important
like slaughtering and filleting the natives
with the knives of their own kindness and patience
was okay so that a new world could flourish

how abhorrent!

and we grow
from zero
to 3/5 of a human negro

it's morbid to torment
a whole people who were peaceful
and now that the ancestry has been contorted
we pour the misery of being poor on America's floor like
agent orange
the porch monkeys

are scorching honkeys
in a metaphorical form of blowing out liberty's torch

and Uncle Sam could care less...
the whole time he has had his money-green eyes on
liberty's breast waiting to walk his dainty boney fingers
across her thighs and up her dress

finger-banging and capitalizing

on what's supposed to be a statue of freedom
is it just me?! cause what you're all seeing as the *freedom figurine*
is actually a state of rigor mortis

what's more important?
the government Doberman pinchers
penny pinching on the coin purses of the unfortunate
for the purpose of waging war for the oil that's stored
beneath the soil of foreign worlds or prisoners of war
becoming collateral damage, now that's horrid!

being raised with the indoctrination of army hatred
this is the master planning behind the bird caging of
nations whose natives are enslaved in these robot graves
that we all play with—it's sordid!

to witness a rising power that should have been historically aborted
the day those three ships came i would have played like i was dr. Kevorkian
vitamin deficiencies like scurvy would have been the least of their worries
and that first greeting "how" would have been more like

POW!

because now
we have acres of lies to plow
to rewrite the stories that have been recorded and now reported as glory
to morph your learning

who shall i consort with when crosses are burning

in the front lawn of this history lesson that's been distorted
for some sort of convergence because this kind of church has
already converted followers who never question and are more than willing to worship

i know for certain when something is told it's as good as sold unless you raise your hand and ask them to un-warp it! please refuse to absorb it or you'll be left splashing in the torrents where teachers are teaching our seedlings to pledge allegiance to a murderous legion who is waving a blood-red white and blue flag flapping in the wind spiked into a whole mountain of history's innocent corpses

and for this—i know that Columbus sailed a warship

sweet guile

America sits
panty less
with her legs open
that's why refugees are willing and rowing
across seas
to plant seeds
not knowing
that the womb they seek is in the belly of the beast

America
with her silly silicon breast
and livid flesh
is a vulture's nest
a candy land of the sweetest guile
cunningly dressed in sparkling sex
and toothpaste smile

America
with her beatniks
then politicians
then endless religions
is a bipolar mental institution
with her lips wrapped around
the barrel of her own constitution

America
miss universe
then miss pornographic
a mind of congested traffic,
i want to touch you
i want to love you
your big cities your big money
most of all the measureless magic
of your new country

ill design

the architecture of this land
comes from an ill design
it was stolen from the free
to make free and then made
slaves out of mine

negro soul and red skin
kick them out and lock us in

pig politicians wearing powdery wigs eat gourmet dishes
and leave poverty remnants of swine
steal something that is free and destroy
tribes with your ill design

red skin and negro soul
invite them back and let us go

gunpowder

i have this fear
that every time i turn my back
my friends smile and bullet shells fall from their mouths

by the time i turn back around
they have neatly wiped the gunpowder from the corners
of their lips
blood drips from their fangs and from their talons

and i'm lovesick
from losing loved ones
lovers and lovebirds to an unloving balance

1,001

i shook 1,000 hands and received 1,000 lies
i've walked 1,000 steps under criticism and
Was stared at and glared at by 1,000 eyes

i spent 1,000 dollars on my girl
She kissed me 1,000 times and
Then crushed my world

i'll give my son 1,000 wisdoms
To use as tools so he can fix
1,001 problems if he's ever fooled

chapter 2
birdcages

fragile things song

(chorus)
fragile things (repeat 2x)
fragile things always flee from me

my endless search for happiness and
all the things i might just miss

for chasing and wasting precious time
the untimely death of righteous minds

working so hard just to attain some things
that one day slip away anyway these fragile things

(repeat chorus 1x)

fragile things

it's like i'm searching for the biggest brightest
whitest gleaming diamond i can find shining
behind the curtains of my mind's hymen blinded
commercials zip by dangling the carrot/karat

and i'm biting the lie spiraling aimlessly through television
skies
flying with an object lust as my thrust...

targeting markets
kneeled in prayer
for American dreams to come true
from 3rd world magic carpets for fragile things
a tinsel jonesing for western garbage

it's like watching bodies breathe sleeplessly without their
hearts in
while corporate conglomerates
sink their teeth in devouring cartilage bone skin
and conscience

creating poverty monsters
who think like this
"since i come from nothing
NOW i want all of it, stick'em up wall street
hand over your wallets"

and nothing is sacred
they're even dangling
platinum crosses
glamorizing coffins

picking monetary cotton
on a plantation of MC-ing – mind control or money
consciousness

reading hieroglyphic carvings
even King Tutankhamen was in on it
filling his tomb with frankincense myrrh and jewelry

the pursuit of happiness has become a pursuit to polish
our inner-hostages

as advertisements nibble at your self-control
like little money hungry piranhas
leaving your heart mangled drifting down
mainstream like a half eaten ravaged carcass

you see, the rich get richer by playing poor
and the poor get poorer by trying to play marvelous
(poppin' collars) buying luxuries first instead
of investing into stock markets or even colleges

i'd/id rather be a square, a peasant
profiting on a wealth of knowledge
than to live my life in circles playing king of the hill
on top of a fragile mountain of material garbage
in love with vaporous mirages

to quote the Marxist
"rise up...you have nothing to lose but your chains"
see it's a spiritual bondage to feign common
when your true identity is more like Siddhartha's

all houses jewels furs cars and even your bodies are perishing garments

so why spend a whole lifetime in the dark starving waiting to dine on such an elusive harvest

half-breed

i feel like all four of my limbs are being torn
like i'm being drawn and quartered
by the force of four horses pulling towards
the four corners of earth's unforgiving fortress

and at her circumference
i'm being encumbered and outnumbered
by a social mass a haphazard disaster
that won't pass without more disaster
i'm too dark for the "whites" and too light for the "blacks"
i'm the new world's new bastard…

i'm fighting alone

and in the misery
of being caught in the guillotine of a race war
so i pace more than any one side has ever paced before

a half-breed
that lacks the vaccine that helps me wax enthusiastically
when fighting back at these savages that attack with
dramatic static
sending disturbing traffic blasting bursting hurting curses
my self worth has surely worsened

or even more so
while being just a brownish torso
the course of this existence has led me to the thoughts
that will complete this sentence

i'm serving undeserving time with each and every line i'm
only partly departing from the garbage they've started
watching them all age in the same ways that candle wax
hardens...slow and molten i'm disheartened with

the races
that are racing
to be the number one race
it's all racist

black or white
the contagion is faceless
so i thank God
or whatever nameless space kid
that decided to place me on the floor
between the addict and basement
so i can see both sides clearly
and maybe change the arrangement
of this deranged slave ship you all are crazed with
the arduous maintenance of rowing together

or maybe i'm just clandestinely destined
to learn a lesson of being pressed in oppression
depressed in a cage of flesh where even angels would fear
to feather
festering secular wings
cross-threaded and embedded
in the very web that was netted
for the enmeshment of ethnic colorings

in the mega erector set of America's malnourishings
her foul milk nurses me with a street lecture the social
pressure to conform

but i'm vexed
because around my darkened red neck
you best bet society could select a neck tie or a noose to be worn

so yeah
i feel like all four of my limbs are being torn cause
i'm stuck in a caste of half slave and half master
so when the opposite side sees the mask that i'm after
they all laugh at the alloying mutation of a half nigger and half cracker

but thank God i am more whim than i am even matter

cause i thought that half and half
was supposed to be the math and havingness of two equal parts
but inside of me there's a revolution
where both sides are loosing
so which color should i be choosing
to color my heart!

blueberry muffin

life can be so sweet
but i still get sour dough
i get so hungry
i could eat my whole family tree
and wash it down with jelly beans

my family genes
seem to have my raggedy pants busting at the seems

cravings for pastas and creams
everywhere i look i see rich & buttery
apple butter scenes marshmallow clouds and blueberry streams

and they don't have me droolin in my sleep
more like they've got me salivating in my dreams

nightmares are me trekking on a gooey treadmill layered in molasses
and my ass is ripping through my jeans and everyone can see

but my buttercup doesn't mind
that i got stretch marks called tiger stripes
and extra skin where it's not needed it's no secret

i gotta a weight problem i'm over weight and i can't wait to eat,
"waiter, bring me my grub!"
like a drug
overeating is serving some unmet need
and now that unmet need is feasting on me

i'm a glutton
with a cereal bowl sized belly button
an egg mc muffin snaggin ham-burglar who be burger grabbin

so greedy
not even the threat of obesity heart disease or diabetes
could slow me down
i'm slow cookin now

would resemble the holiday hog
if you stuck an apple in my mouth
that's what self-esteem tells me

but all jokes and egg yokes aside
this golden arch could give me a swollen heart
if i don't fight

this incredible insatiable
seemingly unstoppable and it feels so impossible
late night appetite

i'm in a food fight
battling hydrogenated mixtures
fructose and rising triglycerides

it's like i am eating myself
it seems i have a recipe
for everything in the fridge & cupboard
and for every can on every shelf
it's a sweet addiction
a slow roasting suicide
a way of cloaking feelings i hide
maybe there really is a hole deep inside of me

that i feel have to shovel mounds of almond joys into
to feel all right

and maybe deep down in this dark hole
my inner-child sits with his back against the wall
hugging his knees sharing his rotten cheese with mice

my real self i've malnourished and deprived
so in my guilt trip i just keep feeding him and spoiling him
as a way of not confronting the real issue

and maybe the real issue is i don't cry
when i'm supposed to i don't get pissed off
and say what i really want to say at that moment
      when i'm pissed off and should
      say what i really want to say
      when i'm suppose to

i swallow my tongue
i treat my real emotions like food & stuff em like a
blueberry muffin

i have a recipe that allows me to take
1 part/what ever food is present and 1 part/emotions
unexpressed
& pop it in my deep dark hole

where i keep my inner child
and let it bake and bake and bake as i swell and swell
and no longer feel so well

i eat until i feel as empty as a doughnut hole
and then eat some more until i'm completely full so that
maybe i'll feel whole

and then out of the blue i eat some more until i feel bluer
than the bluest blueberry

it's scary
cause i see a nation of people who do the same who eat
like pigs who come home from work and eat their stress
who lust for food like food is sex

comfort food my ass...
my hips my chins my chest my flabs
this is uncomfortable

i went from eating to survive
to my eating killing me inside
and i've tried everything from diets to ephedrine highs
i've thumbed endlessly through every magazine
to lose a pound to gain some self-esteem
and in the end it seems the only steam needed is
self-love with a side of belief,
oh yeah...and waiter, please hold the cheese

lost soul

i sat there for centuries sorting
through souls in search of my own;
a quasi-heart hangs inside my chest –
fragile, adamant old-stone

phone conversation with a friend, 10/02/03 10:25am

Friend: hey what up?

Jordan: nothin', what's goin' on with you?

Friend: tryin' to sleep. i got off work at like 2am last night, i had to take two yellow jackets (uppers) to stay awake and i haven't been able to sleep. this stuffs got me wired!

Jordan: damn!

Friend: (switching the subject) i got that book.

Jordan: (feigning omniscience) oh, i know.

Friend: man, you don't know!

Jordan: naw, just playin', what book?

Friend: (chuckling) The Journey of Self-Realization by Paramahansa Yogananda

Jordan: (bragging) ah, yeah i'm halfway through his autobiography.

Friend: (getting focused) but check this out. i'm sitting there reading cause i can't sleep and i read this one part about how a person should meditate every morning to find union with God, so right there i put the book down and began to press my fingers together and they started feeling like they were going into each other. i was thinking naw! am i high. because i knew this wasn't from my own consciousness. remember when you said you had that out-of-body experience?

Jordan: yeah.

Friend: well, what you described is how i felt. (he pauses)

Jordan: (enthralled) i'm listening, go on.

Friend: (whispering) then everything started making sense, like on how i need to stop eating foul foods, drinking and doing drugs, thinking negative thoughts, even cursing - ya know! the whole 9. it was like my flesh was being lectured by my soul.

Jordan: (surprised) damn!

Friend: (confused) what?

Jordan: (proud) that was the deepest thing i ever heard you say! you should write that down.

Friend: what?

Jordan: that your flesh was being lectured by your soul.

Friend: hmm! i've also been having the temptation to smoke again - I was driving around yesterday and i knew i could score some around the corner!

Jordan: (concerned) score some what? i hope you mean some cigarettes?

Friend: naw! that other stuff; the bad stuff.

Jordan: well i pray that you don't.

Friend: oh! i know.

double-barreled bible

united states of mind

i am not the void of all color
        nor am i the absence of light
i am the voice that echoes from Capitol Hill
        August 28, 1963 – that reaches for
the ears of all infinity

i am mutiny in the name of love
        and Webster's definitions are not enough
descriptions to paint the vast spectrum of my eyes

i have made the transition from slave to master
        and in the process have resurrected my tongue
and have come to the memory that this life has just been
another
        chrysalis, eternity's mistress

i am the gold
        that shines beside
mummy wrapped skulls
        in pyramids divine
i invite you to tomb raid my truths

i am the sideways head with inflated cheeks
        blowing Niles of sax vibrations
melodically swaying the jezebel's hips as she moves
smoothly
        against a twilight the color of ripened blackberries
and bizarre cola!

people see me and see the blossom of a seed
        from a strange fruit hanging fleeing

emancipating liberating but still bleeding- i am
        a soul sipping from the fountain marked colored
and in this fountain i don't find youth

instead i find truth and i understand that
        all water flows from one stream and all life grows
from one dream
therefore there can be no separation no segregation
        your attempts are futile – so together we bleed

i stand here as a tool for the cosmos to stare
        my eyes shimmer over a coffee river
these differences have been formed out of a history of
fears

i can't be muted
        i'm undisputed i'm uniting my lost states of mind
i am the music i am the wine
        and the first colonies were built upon the broken
hopes of negro spine!
slave jiggaboo coon nigger even tom
        yes! i have transcended no longer offended those
shackles are gone

i can't be muted
        i'm undisputed i'm uniting my lost states of mind
i am faith i have escaped i am the leap from water to wine
        i am not the void of all color
nor am i the absence of light
        i am black

idyll of Vegas

my eyes dilated
and were then sucked in
by the mystique and wonders of Vegas

there were slot machine zombies
soaking and spitting crisp dollars
in and out of their pores movie-like

mobs and flocks and swarms of souls
gathered crossing at intersections
dragging themselves staggering through
smut infested gutters

there were dimensions and dimensions
of lights and lights illuminating the thick pearly air
slick building sides lacquered sidewalks
and new eyes and defined bone structures

i stood there spying on the leaders and followers

there were pale streams and blankets of cigar smoke
hovering smoothly over fancy mannequins gambling
flipping over jacks and aces with expensive manicures

there were trains and trains of waitresses with more
bucks in their breast than in their brains – sex on the
beach
long island ice teas and bells and horns and whistling all
parading in your ears

there was fluorescent insignia fighting for your eyes
surrounding you at every corner every angle swallowing
you with an electric tongue and ecstatic throat
a million dull quarters dropped and a million cigarettes
were lit all at once

there were Italian chefs with wide grins pouring aromas
and noodles onto the avenues tickling your cravings
luring you in

there were aisles and aisles of brass stemmed chairs
with black leather seats inviting you

there were luminous illusions dancing above
in between the charming designs and on the
glossy faces of your eyes

there were magnificent Asians floating across
the streets walking on time sautéing a fortune

there were stories and stories of glass and brick
kissing the clouds supporting the atmosphere

there were cherry's glowing orange inside of
the cold clammy anxious hands of hustlers

there was a green energy (aura-like) softly dressing
the high walls of the MGM where the lions sleep
and the money comes to life

there was a flood of culture and a blend of nationalities
crossing their fingers counting down swimming in the
spirits breath warmed with liquor

there were motley tapestries strapping the floors and
stacks and stacks of hotel rooms bursting with sex

there were many mariachi advertisements and fiery
fliers of lust clinging to lamp posts up and down

there were coin-filled fountains spitting designs of
water into the airless sweet and black palm trees
stood by gazing at the sweat rolling off absorbing
into silky red

there were a billion buzzes soaring through the
icy night arts and gray brick chimneys blowing
off-white rings around the moon

there were beautiful shoe shiners collecting nickels
decorating the crowd with gleam and mirror shine
selflessly helping new feet find their true path

there were bartenders nourishing casinos flooding cups
the whole city was throbbing

there were golden statues of legends posing inside of
the Motown Café as a large rotating record hung in the
balance
the slot machines continued to mug your pockets

there were jealous stars hanging above the city tops
and large televisions towering the pulsating pavement

there were replicas of world wonders
idling down the side streets
and all of this took place in the warm wind
and in the womb of a blondish sunset

chapter 3
fire poker to the back!

beaten

brandy breath and a burgundy bruise
beaten and burdened and babbling her blues
lies of love lead her to losses cause
lashing lovers were lethal and lawless

my mother and madmen out like militants
dashing the dark side but still dying without diligence
someone slick sucked the science from her soul
i stare a sniper's stare at what the siphon stole

the drinks and drugs drive dreams into diabolical division
the love lacks light on the layers and levels where were
living an asylum of alcoholics and angry angels with no
aim poison with patience paralyzes them and propels me
with pain

i come from bad

i write with the ink from my father's suicide note
so i want to wrap a galaxy size freight train
around mother earth's throat for turning my family tree
into firewood sold for blood money
and leaving my flesh
softly pressed
against the heroin flooded heart
beating beneath my mother's chest

me, i come from bad
i come from three years old and already having a dead dad
and living out of my mother's duffel bag next to Kool
cigarette
packs and a black and gray film case containing the high
powered
memory gag
i do live life mad
cause i strayed from my path
and fell into a crack
and once upon a time i lived on the third floor of a
concrete shack
and watched mom get smacked
with smack

i come from speeding
on a coughing and sneezing
greyhound bus
across America's blue evenings
my country 'tis of thee
broken homes and forbidden lust
bursting veins and exploding brains

in God we trust in God we be dust
in stardust we be like Godliness
but i come from the opposite...
i come from long walks through gardens
past headstones where my memories are
monstrous immortal cause they won't die
they won't leave me to cry
to men mom's love was like wall paper stock
the value wouldn't climb
life's a bitch, a junkie's bad fix
a nympho for crime

i come from family that has passed from cirrhosis
and a therapist prescribing me serotonin in Niagara size
doses
so at age eight i'm learning hate
plagued by fiends of locusts losing their focus
now me and my two brothers we keep moving
and switching schools
while mom plays porcelain mannequin
dressed in lamb's skin
upon barstools
playing fools
with fat pockets
to buy tools
like syringe rockets to blast
into ethereal heavens of outer-scag

i come from bad
i come from ten years old and searching through
our silverware drawer for a spoon without a burnt back!
my dreams went from bright shine to pitch black
from eating at missions and women's shelters and living
in houses that sold crack

i come from the poverty
of a memory
of the lemon tree[1]
existing distantly
but still hitting me
with its sour harvest
so in my power carvings
i try my hardest to reach catharsis
      which means finding freedom through a purging of consciousness
      cause everyone in my life seems to be robbed of it
they hold my vision captive beating and starving it
abusively scarring it
they have failed to learn the science of sacrifice so they
keep revolving in
these six shot pistols
i call statistics
because mathematically without the oil of youthful visions
they'll surely blow their pistons
and give birth to children with vengeance
who are malnourished
and cursed with
being born
in swarms
of slaves
who have lost their essence
and forgotten their ways
and now search for blessings
to build new engines of soul...

my whole tribe comes from cold!
but even while facing these odds or demons or obstacles
i still live life like the unimaginable is possible
i believe that with the right practice nothing can fossil you

double-barreled bible

the only thing stopping you
is a limited sense of self

i sprang from the prosperous loins of wealth
into poverty's slaughterhouse in hell
where promising kids are conditioned with
the habits of parents without visions of
better days and better ways of better living

damn!
sometimes i feel like i have given all that i can give
and still don't live like rose petals on a ridge
that can be hit by forceful winds
and land softly where ever they wish
and not be clouded by the karma of their parent's sins
although i come from bad my aim is for bliss
and i'll be damned if i miss!

[1]the lemon tree (essay)

The lemon tree was a four story lime green project building that sat in the middle of a large dirt field, which was littered with old mattresses that had springs punching through the fabric and strange cotton bleeding around the springs. Old tires, worn and tattered, leaned against ancient trees with wrinkled bark and varicose roots manifesting through cracked soil.

Switchback stairwells reeked of stale urine, and the sweet smell of Thunderbird wine fumed upward from broken bottles that glittered the steps green. At the top of the stair case, aromas of meals seeped underneath doors and filled nostrils with a myriad of herbs and spices; tangy spaghetti sauce and garlic, picante beef and Top Ramen, the scents swirled down the corridors.

As the sun goes down, the scene comes to life. Above, stars sparkle and spangle in a sheet of black sky. Arlene moves outside and rests against the railing. Wearing red high heels with black scuffs all around and stockings with runs in them that cling to her legs all the way up, Arlene has on a gray dress that costs $2 and that is too big for her frail body. She is addicted to crack.

Every morning, when my brothers and i would go outside to play, Arlene would give us some huge doughnuts. They were food bank doughnuts, but we would eat them anyway because we didn't want to upset her. i would usually get the doughnut filled with strawberry jelly. i would lick the filling out first, then eat the rest of the doughnut and follow it with licking the sweet and sticky glaze from the tips of my fingers.

At the lemon tree, there were no bathrooms or stoves in the rooms. Each floor had one bathroom to share. It was much like a gym bathroom, with a big open area with tree style showers and a line of urinals all in one room. In our room, my mom bought a bucket and a toilet seat, rigged a sheet up like a tent, and that was our bathroom. In the hallways, there were red, yellow, blue, and green balloons with heroin in them that junkies would toss when ever Narcs gave chase. Syringes hid in the alley where mountains of garbage bags piled up and beat up cars sat broken down never to be driven again.

Sirens screamed, cops swarmed, hustlers spoke slang, music blared, babies cried, a Muslim chanted, kids ran and laughed, neighbors yelled from floor to floor, and horns and engines from the traffic in the streets filled in the blanks. There were no quiet moments. None.

There was a bloodstain on the top floor. There had been a fight between two men. They were both wearing tank tops, shorts and tennis shoes. One man had a knife and stabbed the other man in the stomach. Blood shot out everywhere, staining the concrete with an expanding puddle of dark fluid. The majority of the blood was cleaned up but nothing could get the stain out of the concrete. To this day, the bloodstain remains in my mind in a memory of the lemon tree.

Jerome's war part I

i can recall my childhood instantly
as if God were vividly
playing motion pictures
aiming to show me through his scriptures
the divine life that i have lost
by all my transgressions
through all of his laws

and i still pray that everyone finds peace
and that no one gets lost like me you see
when i pray
i even pray for my enemy
so that he may one day fight with me
instead of against me

which will strengthen my struggle
to fill what's empty

for the real war is not for diamonds or pearls
it's for saving the world
helping minds unfurl and for properly raising your little girl
when you're lost at sea and she's misguided at shore

now you're unable to be stable
cause growing up has left you insecure

i know the story

mom's beat downs

and overdoses took place
in my young eyes right before me
but i turn to God to reassure
me maybe even restore me

but i can't lie
sometimes i felt that he was gone
and that he was keeping the world turning strictly for my burning
instead of building a stronger path so i could move on

and forget my past
but that's easier said than done
cause i can't seem to forget my past
even though it has passed
it still controls me
every memory a stinging hit
from a whip lashing my back
and no one is there to console me
so when i get angry and shove guns into the mouths of the innocent
that's just me lashing back at the feelings that i can't see
so instead of talking i just react

DAMN!

i'm trying to get free
but the adversary has hidden the shackles deep within me
and nobody's listening

they really think that i love
being out of touch

out of God's clutch
swearing
glaring eyes
shooting hollow points
at anyone who enjoys the sun

but that's not the case
i wasn't always this way
it has taken time and change
to harden my face

forget a mile in my shoes
you would have to live 1000 lifetimes
      through wastelands with youth just as lost as you
        just to feel one icy shard off of the iceberg that
barely compares to my abuse

i AM DEAD!

doctors are glad to sell me pills
      but could care less about what's going on inside of
my head

something is wrong here
i don't belong here
i scream for help and nobody answers
and so wanes my lantern
i miss my original planter
my mother's womb
i wish i could return there soon
as a matter of fact i take that back
i wish i could exist one stage before that!

wounded part II

i know that his mistakes
have set the stakes
      even higher

and now i see Gods
trapped in pigs
      trapped in mud & fire

trapped in the slop in a hog's trough
of a God forsaken Godless
      world of worldly desire screamin' God dammit i'm
trapped

he's up to his chin in sin
blindfolded higher than high with high hopes on tight
ropes
      walking the high wire highly wired

crying out
that the sky is the limit
      and there is no sky

so underneath nothing
a battle between lions and lambs erupts
      but he's tired of fighting and just flat out tired

and i know
i know the place where his soul froze
      & he chose to let go

hiding from himself

swinging at his own shadow
    running from his own eyes cause he sees know
where to go

so now go with me
as i watch his tear laden prayers climb clouds balloon-like
    effervescently and oh so heavenly
        towards a heaven that he doesn't even believe in

he doesn't even believe in his own breathin'
the ebb and flow
    is wretched YO!

and i have even seen'em attempt to snuff out his own
heart beating that's hardly beating

he says "God's heart is deceiving, who drops their
kids off at the park then escapes into the clouds and tells
them to find him in
their own heart! MAN that is misleading!"

and in the dark
outnumbered by demons
    i hear him screamin

so please heavenly father
grant me the most gigantic Wings
    that one can dream up

for i have been whipped
spit on
    and eaten alive

i know the enemy wants
my heart   my smile   my inner child
i would cry a Nile
         but he's even eaten my eyes

wounded
i'm wounded like a Nam veteran missing legs
         who wakes up in the middle of the night
         20 years after the war

cursing and screaming
crying and crawling passed empty bottles of whiskey
         to the bathroom to glance in the mirror

to see if his soul
still holds up his face
         the way it once used to

shell shocked
only i've never been in a war
         and all i know is i don't cry anymore

my legs are ok
yet i'm unable to walk a way
         without feeling wounded

yellow woman

an orchestra of teeth
without a song

in someone's backyard
a spill of blood is illumined
by ambient light

a revolver sinks in the dew of
their lawn

syringe and crucifix
east then west

she stares at the oblong shape
in the reflection of a spoon

passing overhead –
clouds: albino, cocaine, off,
all white on sharp blue
she stares

a 2nd grader peeks in a bedroom
where a yellow woman sleeps
with invisible floating eyes…

yeah…
her eyes

i remember now
they were abandoned by her soul

in a dream she witnessed life

double-barreled bible

colored with wild graffiti of:
money green
cocaine white
heroin brown
blood red
jaundice yellow
pussy pink
nigger black
revolver gray
and faint traces of holy bible gold
a pretty girl trapped inside of a diamond
that's why her eyes were orphaned her soul could no
longer raise them on its own

lighthouses

in the distance
she sees a floating lighthouse perched in the clouds
as a small child drifting away in fantasy

while grimy men
with filthy minds
shove dirty fingers down her panties

slimy men
who sit on stoops & get stupid with joints and booz
ugly dudes who spout out with nothing to talk about
      losers with nothing and no one to lose

discussing and cussing bout
their losing battles and new shoes

and speaking of speaking things into existence
her every sentence grew roots

a wild flower in her youth
my mother's nature is fragrant proof
of one who has tamed the spooks

i used to think that i was a hard-knock hard luck bastard
that was doomed to have it hard left in hard headed hands
spur of the moment plans shelters and soup kitchens

i was just bitchin
pissin & moaning

hell most of Africa's got it badda

than more than half of America's 'ghetto' born rappers
who rap about slums and not having shit

how blasphemous
i know better now that
i was breast fed by an angel named Naomi
who has lived in hell her whole entire life

the edges of her feathers are still charred
and every now and then i gaze at orange embers burning slowly
a mere mortal impressed by her power
a collection of miniature lighthouses surrounds her
and its like these little figurines are reminding her to keep reaching for freedom no matter how far away that freedom may seem

there are bridges burning all around her smoldering
there are pimps & pushers pushing death-mobiles
bragging about their crushed velvet and peppermint gum
poppin ho's all around her
     sons of throw-away guns who aim to paint the town red
         life spans like shooting stars from being stabbed in a bar
         to lost tribes raised in a barn by speeding bullets
all of this all of the time whizzing all around her

as she hop scotches the lime colored chalk sidewalks
i plead with her a blood curdling scream
retreat & don't look back!

cause you are running from a monster
     a grenade-brain, soul like a flickering light bulb

       rockin a trench coat with your memories like stolen
gold watches
       hanging in neat rows on the lining ready to crush
your lighthouses
       and hammer the sun into the blackness

Monster
like a wolf in flashy sheep clothing a thief wearing God's
robe but with trashy cheap sewing
a monster of frost and snow

and i know you want to climb
that long winding stairwell into the sunshine
even if there are a million stairs to scale

even if every muscle in your aging body is burning
and your legs are aching and sore begging you to stop

i know that you would brush it off
inhale the clouds and keep movin'
cause dad is waiting at the top to kiss you on your
forehead

a gentle shepherd
patiently standing by watching his sheep leap one by one
into flames from cliffs & rooftops
has an eternal kiss for your forehead
so fluff your wool and keep your cool

Dear Mom, life is but a dream...

chapter 4
meditating on the sun

fortune

deep beneath the sands of my flesh
beneath my chest
there has been a longing in my soul
and that longing has created pressure
and that pressure has turned my heart into a precious stone
the dumb luck of stumbling upon something rare where i thought there was nothing that could be touched but air, you are my everything and i vow from this day forward to honor you as such you are my sustenance and your words are my clouds like stairs that i climb when i feel that i just can't breathe without you by my side...
my lungs are run away balloons in vanishing skies
our eyes sparkle like jewels
like torches lighting up tombs
filled with gold
beneath the sands of my flesh
i'm filled with gold
beneath my skin
my spirit blows breath against my ribs
like winds to wind chimes
i am filled with your song
our hearts are brightened rubies
pulsating jewelry
as we walk in unity
your hand in my palm
(forever) like a diamond
you are like a diamond
you shine even when in a dark cave
and 10x brighter when the sun bathes
there are not enough treasures on earth that compare to

my wealth
there are not enough nerves in my words to describe how
i feel
i'm on wings
and it's beyond butterflies in my stomach
it's complex it's in my solar plexus
and i only know this
because i only notice
when i'm next to you
what i'm trying to say is that i treasure you
i do

she's fly

she's fly
and not just like slang in '85
she's fly like angel's wings on babies
dangling from clouds in Raphael's famous painting
fly like Michelangelo's hanging masterpiece God's creation

and she speaks the language
of eternity with love skinny dipping
from the tip of her tongue she could be the one
i've been waiting for and possibly the one that i came for

cause i swear i would harvest every star
from every galaxy for her i would and if i could
i would scribble both of our names in the moon
and trace them with a heart

together there forever never to be touched by weather

versus the world that we live in
that seems to be withering away
and falling apart all around us but we bloom
two of a kind working in unison like one mind

she is my queen
and i am her worker bee
building a honeycomb in her bee hive
pollinating patiently
cause this worker bee be longing for her inside

and yes

i know that that metaphor could have been written by a child
but the truth is she makes me smile
so my youth is let loose and running wild
i'm feeling the way i used to feel so its worthwhile

you see i went from walking on water to completely drowning

to finally finding someone who keeps my heart pounding

she glows
she flies
and i don't care why
cause here in the afterlife
she conquers the heavens soaring through the skies
apparently transparent
blending in with the horizon
or even disguised in
the wings of butterflies
1000 watts brighter than fireflies
a flying angel with bonfires like burning eyes
into infinity she glides divine
she's levitating in my mind

fly
above the mountains
above the falcons
and beyond the clouds
her aura could cool the sun down
and she gallops through my dreams never touching ground

haunting me peacefully

it's the most profound feeling
and i just want to be part of her flight
tonight right now i want us to leave our bodies
together and never return to fly

forever beyond
forever beyond
forever beyond this lifetime

cause i might have found love this lifetime
i might have finally found what i came searching for
when i crept into this lifetime
and if we fly away now love could be ours forever

then i could sever my mind
forever from my body
building wings on my soul
to unfurl and leave this world

having never lost love
and having only lost myself in love
with her i am in love with her

i'm in love with her wings
i'm in love with her dreams
and i'm in love with the dreams she has for me
to fly

insatiable

flirting gambling basking
in the shiny loot of your sexy soul while
shimmering dancing nourishing
ourselves with invisible fruits that
blossom glow and ignite bonfires in our
gentle eyes as a seed of love snakes
through the soil in the green gardens
of our insatiable minds in the odd stare
of a glass moon hovering inside an awkward
reverie that sexily cools the bizarre twilight
within forever i am you

magnanimous you

you
the speech
the fire
the cosmic love
that free-falls through and interjects the stagnant norm

you
the sharp-eyed beauty
the water
the golden dust
blowing and dressing the winds in deserts of places of
minds long extinct

you
the jeopardy
the earth
the bronze shadow outlined in yellow
dancing a wild dance of life and peace in the jasmine
chambers of my nucleus

you
the sapphire kiss of creation
the breath
the dazzling furnace of time
gliding at a low speed robed in velvet and jazz to nourish
me

your music is my womb

postcards of heaven

you are forever speaking about
postcards of heaven with no return address
      and i think that is beautiful

you have lost philosophies
      to remind the world of... like how unconsciousness
is at the root of slavery
      and i believe that is true

i am really in love with your
      thrift-store-robed spirit
      that carries a pistol grip King James version of the
dead sea scrolls
      you float inside of your body separate
      from your mind with hues of red roses
      moving rain like romance

i love you...
      because you never sleepwalk into cabarets
      even though the notes playing inside are a deluge
of your beauty in sound form

Dear Maisha,
      You are the highest obelisk.

world hunger

i only want to love her
because i'm tired of being outnumbered
i'm tired of freefalling upwards
in between the stars & clouds just to speak above the thunder
her love can feed the poor i have discovered
she is a World Wonder
and i have a world hunger
i am completely impoverished until i can love her

meditation with Rama

in a dream
i see Rama chimerically gliding towards
me over a field of darkened rose petals as old as the earth
itself

her dainty feet
don toe jewelry
and they dangle at the bottom of a bright saffron robe

behind her
there's a swirling pink sky on fire with her aura
i'm in the half lotus

she has eyes like resplendent dandelions
that chisel at the ceramic of my unwanted habits
when the world curls its serpentine finger at me

she is a flower that has been pressed and dried
between the pages of every book ever written
by all the prophets and sages absorbing their words
and leaving her fragrance a divine exchange and
holy engagement

i say we all hold hands and leap...

chapter 7
transformation

clairvoyance

i have trained my eyes to bend corners

mind power

your mind
is achieving

the thoughts
that it's
receiving

powered
by believing

your world
was once
a seedling

in the garden
of your dreaming

gigantic

last night i dreamt that i was a giant

i tiptoed over bridges and ponds
swatted the clouds and twirled
my fingers around clusters of stars

i awoke to discover myself

as tall as the universe is high
as deep as the universe is wide

and as rich
as the universe is

awakening

screaming at God in the mirror!
i spotted the jewel of knowledge
      upon a mountain top
      hell of a climb
           but now the jewel is mine
      the jewel is mind
      with this dying eye
           i can see a beautiful world now-
                a precious side to life emerging
all the riddles and all my pain have been my creation,

    alone
i know now that i have always existed,
           outside of myself, waiting to remember
disconnecting-
from the world's fruits:
           radio
           sex
           tv
           whisky – and other material derangement
to unveil a higher self has been out of my reach
until now

      for years i would fan my soul
      with wisdom-stained papyrus scrolls – in search of
the law

      now i bow with my spirit so that i may awaken and
self realize:
      replace weakness with strength
           trade lust for love
           sacrifice greed to be more giving

restore a wandering mind with careful attention

and find myself a being
carved from radiant illumination

the light of God

i too am the lotus

i too am the lotus

calm as one thousand Jain monks steeping like tea in a state of samadhi

the truths of the universe are all my offspring

if my endless petals cease then my reincarnation will spring from my seeds
i too am the lotus

earth plus air plus fire plus water equal my flesh
i, the lotus, am the conqueror of death

i too am the lotus
that bends for the wind as if its course were an inevitable prophecy

fasting, unfolding endlessly, always beginning

not a body passing through life but life passing through a body

immortal

i too

am the lotus

light

as an offering

i will give you
eons of bouquets of constellations
and the sunray's progeny of illuminations
vineyards of solar systems i'll harvest for you

my fetish is feathered
       with thoughts of you

the way the sunlight travels at light speed
                                   ever so lightly

on ether to reach your
incandescent complexion
as soothing winds pass
gently through heavens
through strands of your hair
that's sun-kissed and
softly dressing your divinely charged aura

and i stare

i stare at things
i know are not there
beautiful things
that are just chimerical carvings
of my mind's imaginings
your love must be maddening

because i detect

dimensions of rhythms and out of worldly prisms
that send me rising past the zenith like phoenix
beyond suns that have fully risen and you gleam and you
glisten

like the reflection of
starlight multiplied by twilight
then magnified 1,000 times
off of the mirror that touches my soul's vision

it's blinding
brightly lighting
new designs of lightning
inside of my enlightening

it creeps and it seeps
      into the depths
where my heart is encrusted with darkness
and i'm telling you now if no one else has we all are truly
starlit beauties

that come without warning
an aesthetic storming warming
every single one of my infinite life's journeys
transforming my yearnings

of old paths i used to seek
i'm dropping the skin now
forever living within now

no longer holding on to the things
i know i could never keep like precious
jewels or precious loot or even more precious
above all is the most precious side of you

double-barreled bible

i sometimes pursue
into the affluent
treasury of my reveries
in search of a rebirth that will measure me
timelessly and ever new and i'll find that when we are one

enamored with
glamorous light
that is a phantom's kiss
from lantern lips

because
we are all
the products of
stars and suns

we are all
the products of
stars and suns

and you see things
the same way i believe
and i conceive us to be

slivers and shards of the broken glass of the omni-window
that is God's heart

photosynthesis of art
you fill me with light

and i'm high on life
like she be bringing me bouquets of poetic poppies
i'm like up late at night slinging kilos of immortal stardust
to the heartless for their catharsis cause it's marvelous

to watch life without watching our watches

our nature is clock-less

my eyes
slowly skim and skip across
blackened oolong colored skies i'm lost
when the moon blows me her silver kisses
i'm drunken with moonshine inundated
with ambience eternally fermenting in light's chrysalis
it takes discipline and focus to sit indian-style or full lotus
while flames and smoke roll and float
upwards from your aura's wholeness

sacrifice and boldness
are the only ways to break the mold
holding control of your soul
that's carved from the same substance as light

spaced out! and star struck!
i'm in love with light

song of the God Self

sometimes I'm blind with Eden
when flying towards the sun
and her corona is blood red
like licorice is and I get burned
like Icarus did
when attempting to return to the one
it's a treasure hunt
it's like finding a map that leads to a map and that map
leads right back to the first map and reads "be still"
it's journey uphill
it's a quest over a bridge built from last words from
prophets
it's similar to fireflies that bounce off of street lights in
search of the sun
it's bullets to a gun
it's the bank robbers cry when he commands bankers to
"reach for the sky"
or "put 'em up high" to touch the most high
this is about wealth
this is about finding yourself
about a great thief
who wouldn't steal cheese from mice
who puts the lit moon in the night
he who through my dreams witnesses me fly my heart like
a kite
on winds that I pray will carry my imagination from here
to heaven
like heaven is some sort of imagined nation created by the
thoughtful

dreams of eternal beings and I would shed my skin this moment
if it means that I can spend the rest of eternity keeping paradise
spinning space
the truth is I believe my father and I share the same face
behold!
God is the glow in my soul
the light of my enlightenment
the rays of my radiance
the treasure that I've been seeking
God is my gold

final note

art of language

i speak dreams into existence or objects into spaces
a man of my word i represent the art of language
in an unspeakable age
where tongues are misplaced and taste
has become so tasteless
where sex sells the soul
& war crime pays and paves ways
for estranged slaves
who could've of escaped but get raped
then feed their babies the same hate
that they were raised with
self hate is the deepest kind of hatred
deeper than that self hate is the only type of hatred
i speak of modern day enslavement
and hearts of ice zooted up nights
zombie brothers and mummified mothers
who no longer call each other lost in the struggle
juggling their bills with bloody knuckles
breast and honey suckle violence and crack pipes
internal ice & eternal spiritual fights
i'm talking about war for gutter folk
and those of us who rose from dust to bloom
to whom a food stamp was a magic carpet ride
through the grocery store or war for kids
who came from nothing-was given nothing
but found that missing something
and turned life into so much more and now soar
i represent all that is pure
the bridge between rich and poor

the time machines and the timeless wings that traverse hell
prophets or poets who lift spells and dispel the fog
mothers who uplift, it is to you i blow a kiss
and mimic God's greatest gift
i represent free thinkers who float the high seas aimlessly
who set no sail, who know thy self who walk on waves crazily in bliss
who know they know nothing of everything
and so wander the earth speechless and soul adrift
this is intimate, with my words to you i blow a kiss...

glossary

(words defined in order of appearance)

mission statement
sever- divide or separate; to cut off
reverence- the act of adoring or showing respect
bestow- to give formally or officially as a gift
pious- holy, godly

picket sign
Molotov cocktail- a glass bottle with a cloth fuse and flammable liquid used as a makeshift bomb, name comes from a Russian political leader, Molotov
shrapnel- the metal fragments of an exploding bomb or grenade
alchemy- a power or process of transforming something common into something special
tenement- run-down apartment house in a poor section of a city
marbling- the livid appearance of dead skin before it decays
panhandling- asking for spare change
onyx- jet black; a semi-precious gem
miasmic- any evil influence or poisonous atmosphere
noxious- corrupting; harmful to other things

Columbus sailed a warship
sage- profoundly wise man
abhorrent- disgusting; repelling
contorted- bent or twisted out of shape
agent orange- a herbicide containing trace amounts of the toxic contaminant dioxin used in the Vietnam War to defoliate forests where the enemy hid

dainty- elegant
rigor mortis- stiffening of the body after death
horrid- horrible
indoctrination- to instruct in learning, principles
sordid- dirty, filthy; morally degraded
Dr. Kevorkian- a.k.a. dr. death, he specialized in euthanasia or assisted suicide
morph- to transform; change shape
consort- to associate with or harmonize
convergence- to bend together, to tend toward one point
torrent- a turbulent swift-flowing stream; a heavy downpour of rain

sweet guile
livid- lacking color; discolored angry
guile- deceitfully clever; a trick or strategy

fragile things
hymen- a tissue that partly or completely covers the external vaginal orifice; sign of virginity
carrot/karat- the vegetable/used to express the fineness of gold or weight of diamonds
tinsel- thin, glittering metallic material in strips or sheets, used for showy decoration
jonesing- street slang for a strong craving, usually for sex or drugs
conglomerate- a combination of dissimilar things; a company formed by merger with or acquisition of several companies in widely different industries
hieroglyphics- the pictographic writing system of ancient Egypt
King Tutankhamen- King of Egypt during XViii (18th) dynasty, ca. 1350
frankincense- an aromatic gum resin obtained from

double-barreled bible

African and Asian trees used as incense and in perfumes
myrrh- an aromatic gum resin also obtained from African and Asian trees used as incense and in perfumes
id- in Freudian theory, the unconscious part of the psyche that serves as the source of instinctual impulses and demands immediate satisfaction of primitive needs
vaporous- insubstantial or vague substance; extravagantly fanciful
mirages- something illusory or insubstantial; an optical illusion
Marxist- adherent to the political and economic philosophy of Karl Marx where class struggle plays a central role in understanding society's allegedly inevitable development from oppression under capitalism to a socialist and ultimately classless society
feign- to give a false appearance of; to fake a move or appearance
Siddartha- Buddha's name, Siddartha Guatama, ca. 500 BC
elusive- escaping; difficult to define or describe

half-breed
encumber- to hinder; to put a heavy load on
haphazard- accidental; by chance
guillotine- apparatus for beheading humans
wax- to increase in size, power, or degree; moon phase progressing from new to full
contagion- communication of disease by contact; a communicable disease; corrupting influence
arduous- difficult task, testing the power of endurance
clandestine- secret, concealed; done in secret, often to conceal improper purpose
secular- worldly rather than spiritual; not bound by religious constraints
enmeshment- entangled

vexed- mad; brought suffering to
alloying- weakened purity with other elements; combining elements
revolution- the overthrowing of a power; the turning around

blueberry muffin
salivating- drooling; to secrete saliva from the mouth
molasses- the dark thick gooey syrup that you get when you refine cane sugar
obesity- overweight
cloaking- to disguise or mask something
ephedrine- a plant once used in now banned weight loss pills

lost soul
quasi- almost, seemingly; prefix meaning "to some degree"
adamant- any hard or unyielding substance; stubbornly unyielding

phone conversation with a friend
omniscience- all knowing
enthralled- captivated

united states of mind
void- empty; eastern religious concept of nothingness
August 28th, 1963- date of Dr. Martin Luther King, jr.'s "i have a dream" speech
Nile- river in E. Africa
strange fruit- metaphor from female jazz singer Billy Holiday describing black people who had been lynched
futile- hopeless

undisputed- can't be argued with, no contest
transcended- to rise above

idyll of Vegas
idyll- a descriptive verse or prose of a place
dilated- to enlarge
mystique- mystical aura of something or someone
insignia- a mark; sign or badge
luminous- something shining bright; radiating, glowing
motley- diverse elements; multi-colored
mariachi- traditional Mexican dance music

beaten
diligence- persevering; attentive care
siphon- tube used for the suction of liquids; moving liquids by siphoning
diabolical- wicked; having characteristics of the devil
asylum- institution for care of the aged, blind, orphaned, or insane; a place offering protection and safety
propel- to drive onward

i come from bad
cirrhosis- inflammation and disease of the liver caused by alcoholism
serotonin- pleasure chemical in the brain
ethereal- light, delicate, heavenly, spiritual
scag- street name for heroin
purging- emotional cleansing; push out
vengeance- revenge
essence- true nature
prosperous- thriving; wealthy
karma- destiny by past actions

the lemon tree (essay)
varicose- abnormally swollen veins
manifesting- showing; bringing into existence
myriad- many
corridors- long hallways
spangle- to sprinkle or strew with shiny objects

Jerome's war
divine- proceeding from a god; a god
transgression- to break a law; to commit a sin
unfurl- to reveal, unfold
console- to give comfort
adversary- enemy
wanes- dimming; moon phase progressing from full to new

wounded
laden- loaded down; burdened with
effervescently- bubbling upward
snuff- inhale through the nose; extinguish
wretched- poor, pitiful

yellow woman
illumined- glowing; enlightened
oblong- long shape
albino- lacking pigmentation, usually expressed in white or nearly white animals
jaundice- abnormal condition characterized by yellowness of the eyes, skin, and urine which is caused by the bile in the blood; exhibiting prejudice, hostility, or envy

lighthouses
perched- to stand or sit in an elevated place
blasphemous- profane

fortune
vow- promise
sustenance- nourishment
solar plexus- nerves meeting between the stomach and heart; guts

she's fly
transparent- see through
levitating- floating in mid-air
crept- to creep, to advance slowly to a point

insatiable
insatiable- unable to be satisfied
basking- exposed to pleasant heat; to take pleasure or satisfaction

magnanimous you
magnanimous- high-minded, noble; above pettiness
interjects- interrupts; to insert between
stagnant- not flowing; foul or stale; lacking vitality
jeopardy- risk
nucleus- any body or thing that serves as the center for growth or development

postcards of heaven
hue- color; the property of color that ranges from red through violet
cabaret- restaurants providing dancing and entertainment
deluge- a flood
obelisk- a tall four sided stone pillar with a pyramidal top

world hunger
impoverished- deprived of power; poverty stricken

meditation with Rama
donning- wearing; putting on
saffron- deep yellow or orange color; aromatic yellow herb used in cooking and dyeing
half lotus- meditation position
resplendent- shining brilliantly; dazzling in appearance
serpentine- snake-like

clairvoyance
clairvoyance- seeing in the mind what is going to happen; foresight

awakening
unveil- to uncover
wisdom-stained-papyrus-scrolls- the bible
illumination- lighting up; to find wisdom

i too am the lotus
lotus- flower with seemingly endless petals; a meditation position in Eastern religions
Jain Monk- a monk who takes up no dwelling so as not to displace animals from their homes, they also wear masks over their mouths so as not to kill bugs by swallowing them
Samadhi- state of God union; collected in the mind
inevitable- unavoidable
prophecy- prediction of the future
fasting- self-denial; going without necessities, often food

light
eon- long period of time
progeny- offspring
incandescent- glowing white with heat
aura- distinctive air or atmosphere surrounding a person; the soul

chimerical- imaginary; consisting of mixed genetic composition
prism- object that disperses light
zenith- point of the heavens directly over a person's head
phoenix- mythological bird that rose from its own ashes
encrusted- encased; outwardly covered
aesthetic- sensitive to beauty; philosophy of beauty
affluent- abundant- prosperous
reverie- lost in thought; a dream
enamored- in love
kiss- when lips come together to separate bodies and merge the souls
shards- slivers of something broken into fine pieces
omni- all
photosynthesis- process used by plants to convert sunlight into usable energy
catharsis- purging of emotions through expression
oolong- a brown or black Asian tea
inundated- flooded
ambience- pervading atmosphere; mood
chrysalis- cocoon; metaphoric phase such as between caterpillar and butterfly

song of the God Self
corona- concentric circles seen around the sun or the moon
Icarus- character from classical mythology who was warned not to fly to close to the sun with his wings that he had fashioned from wax and feathers
quest- a search to obtain something
prophet- a person who speaks for God
paradise- heaven

Acknowledgements

In 2004 life found me pushing a boulder up a mountain, and without the love and support of the following people, that boulder would have crushed me and the dreams...

To my Mom, you taught me to survive, to create, to taunt my dreams so that they chase me rather than the other way around, for miracles across the states, for raising three knuckle-heads with your own loving bare knuckles, you have always been my hero I may not have said it enough but it's true, I modeled myself the best that I could after your dreams and visions. I love you Moma, you are God's most beautiful earth angel, flaws and diamonds perfectly united -- your heart is a planet.

To Paris for the fell swoop, for mega-feathers all around, for resuscitation, revival, for bringing me back, you are the perfect verse, prose in motion, soul of the rose, our names etched in the frame work of forever, olive juice. To my son David for keeping my Visa current in Imagine Nation, for vocals that make angels cry, for songs that open hearts, for making me a proud father.

To my brother Jerome for taking the brunt of it, for flying kites in the storm, for keeping a golden heart in the wastelands, for armor. To my sister Shanna, whom I have never met in person and just so happened to meet in a poetry chat room as fellow poets, bizarre true story. Uncle Lou for teaching me that being a Man simply means having poise. For my cousin, Autumn Dawn, for the first college degree in our family, for torch bearing, you're lifting us all up and were watching. To my cousin Marcus Davis aka Modest Monk aka M.O.D.E.S.T. aka Most Our Dreams Eventually Shine Through, for road doggin to gigs in and out of state, late night highway ciphers, all for the love of art and stealing good folks' hot dogs. Orion Baker for meeting me at the splatter-spot, for orientation, for Fort Jesus and Hard Times, I think your height has something to do with levitation. Michelle Price for everything and MORE, for 2004, for enlarging me with the confidence to put on the gloves and fight for my dreams, for building me up.

Ernie Chapin you have been a Teacher, a Guide, a Peaceful Warrior, a Friend and a Father to me, there is absolutely no way that I could ever repay you for all that you have done for me. Dianne Shepherd you have been in my life ever since I could remember, you rescued my family the best that you could, when nobody else would you opened my door. Mareesa Henderson for Unity in the Community, for rising like Phoenix, for distorted dance moves that never catch on. Ellen Tomaszewski for nurturing all of my ideas, for Rivers of Ink, for RAF, and for picking up the phone to hear me rattle off plans, plots schemes & dreams like gravel in a pop can.

To Amy Bond for shelter, for culture, for piano riffs like fading stars and Mano Chao. Adam Partridge for requiems of tap-dancing, Yogananda and Tullies. For my long time friend James Nemeth for enthusiasm like rocket fuel it always made me believe, for honorary Tacoma press passes, for 10 U-Haul trucks one summer, for friendship. Cristina Orbe cyber friend, fellow sky walker, thank you for encouraging me to just spit it out.

Mike and Patty Briggs for the quote, and for the incredible honor of dinner with greatness. To Dave Abbott aka Sensei Uncle, for pen fire, for courage to just be self, for Shakespeare notes. Amy Davis for wine education, and pronouncing sommelier? AJ at Power 99.1 for 9 holes, for air waves, for music.

Twa-le Abrahamson, for social consciousness, for Inner Tribal Beat, for air waves. Pat Bacily for radio at 5 floors up. Sysommay Kaiphanliam at skaiphotography.com for the windy alley and beauty in the rubble, for the ash photograph, for Pho and Long Green beans. Maisha Christian for the baptism with tears in the desert year 2000, for prayers like stairs, for wound wash, for Saints and Angels. Erick Peterson for heralding my poetry throughout Eastern Washington, for drinks and possibly Hot Pot one day.

To Kimberly Harden for carving your friendship into my network, for links that turn into success, for Richard Hugo House. Bart Baxter for the sweat stained stage two years in a row, for seeing my mission so clearly, for slam.

Karen Yeskavage, Tony and the Students at CSU Pueblo, CO thank you for the journey in Red Clay Everywhere, for Poor Richards, for Garden of the God's, for Mud Castles and home-made bread, for Manitou outside theatres, for Sea-Side. For Dalores S. and the Students at Every Child has Hope, St. Louis, MI, this is written for all of you.

Kimberly Moorer-Perry thank you for the ride home, for the tremendous love and support, for seeing the vision. Mal Stewman from the Center for Student empowerment for invites galore, college campus love and mass appeal. Ryan Jander from Eclectic Approach for the creative writing sessions, brainstorms and food drive. Scott Wells, for massive creativity, for our Shawshank-esque introduction, for illusions of caged birds – thank you.

To Travis Senger for Howl, for broadening my vision of poetry. Paul Angiano for the website & Candy L. Norman for camaraderie with ROI and RAF, for eGuidance. Rajnii Eddinns, Matt Gano, Danny Sherrard, Kammeron Brown, poetry Gods, cloud kickers, for the birth pains of Billowing Words. For Yirim Seck and Inye Wokoma for Light, One Verse and The Key.

Thank you all so much for believing in me, for our conversations, for opening up your homes and hearts to me, for sticking by my side and or giving space when things got bumpy.

If I have forgotten anybody I apologize sincerely.

Metaphors be with you,

Jordan

From Upcoming Works by Jordan Chaney

***Mighty Peasant* Spoken Word Album by Jordan Chaney NOW AVAILABLE!**

Mighty Peasant is a spoken word poetry album injected with raw spiritual consciousness, stardust, and gunpowder.

***

Rocket Fuel for Dreamers by Jordan Chaney

Rocket Fuel for Dreamers is a FREE pocket book of motivation, inspiration, and one love poem for anyone who has lost momentum in life.

"Open as wide as you wish the furnace of your heart,
of your passion, and shovel in piles of coal,
take the firewood of your visions, of your dreams
and throw them in, stoke it with mediation and focus,
and at last drench your heart's wildest desires
with rocket fuel and ignite the reality you truly seek."
     -from *Rocket Fuel for Dreamers*

***

Fly by Jordan Chaney. *Fly* is a book of love and imagination poems.

"I want you to know that you are adored
that you are truly heaven's blessed ornament
the master's masterpiece and it's worlds beyond
anything like worship I would battle a warship
armed with nothing more than an ore for you…"
-from *Fly*

***

P.U.R.E. Teaching: Motivating the Unmotivated
By Ernie Chapin and Jordan Chaney

P.U.R.E. Teaching: Motivating the Unmotivated
is a teacher's and student's true story.

"A clean slate was on the horizon; I got the strong sense that I could quite possibly turn my life around, that it wasn't too late there was still hope for me. That day I made a new set of decisions, a decision to stop blaming everything and everyone and most importantly the decision to try."
-From *P.U.R.E. Teaching*

***

For more information, visit Jordan's website at www.billowingwords.com